Design and Make
CARDS

Helen Greathead

Smart Apple Media

Contents

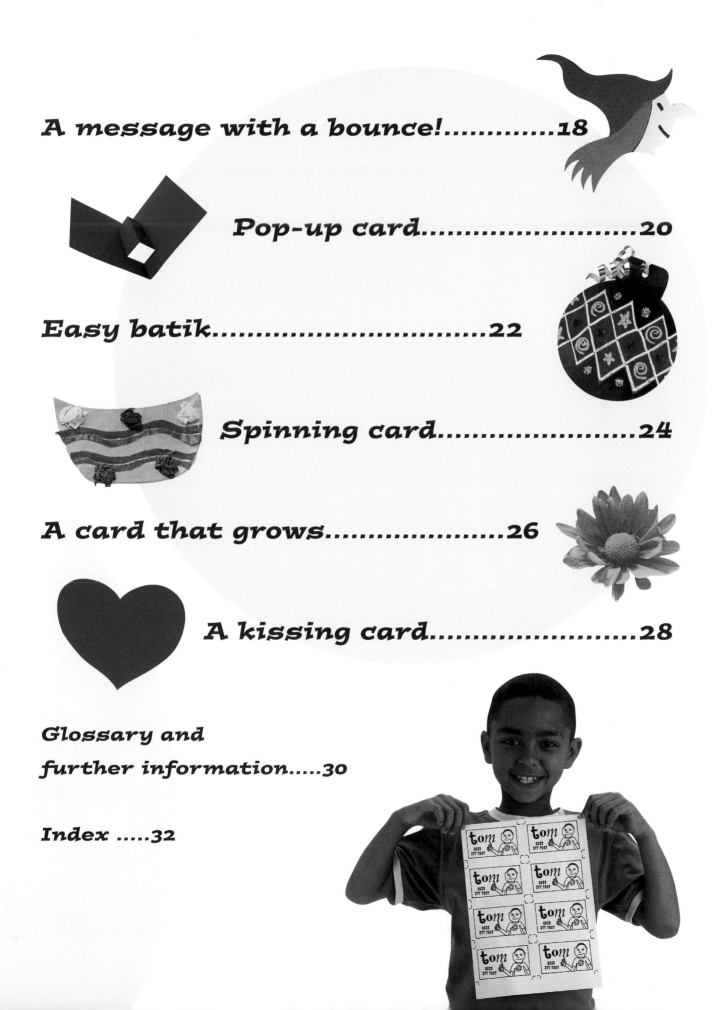

A card for every occasion

Do you like giving and receiving cards? People have been sending cards for centuries, but in the last 150 years, they have become big business around the world. In this book, we show you how to make cards with things you can find around your home. There are ideas for pop-up cards, fabric cards, and even cards inspired by nature.

Valentine's verse

The earliest European greeting cards were Valentine's Day (February 14th) cards. Back in the Middle Ages, lovers used to sing Valentine's verses to each other. But after 1400, they started to send messages in cards. These were made by hand and often were very fancy! Some cards were folded and cut into lace patterns; others had stenciled pictures on them.

Kate Greenaway

Kate Greenaway was a children's author and illustrator, but she also designed greeting cards. Her first Valentine's card, published in 1868, sold 25,000 copies!

Christmas cards

In 1843, Englishman Henry Cole sent the first Christmas card. He wanted to remind his friends to think about the poor during the festive season. So the first Christmas card was also the first charity card. In the United States, the first Christmas card was produced in 1851, but the idea took another 20 years to catch on. New printing techniques, and the arrival of the penny post system in 1873, started a card-sending trend that is still growing!

Celebrations

Today, people in countries all over the world send cards to celebrate birthdays and festivals. Many people send cards for the New Year, and for their own religious festivals, such as the Hindu festival of Diwali or Jewish Hanukkah. Now, we can even send e-cards for every occasion!

Using your imagination

In this book, we encourage you to look at store-bought cards and cards from around the world for inspiration, and to think about ways of making your own. Use the techniques we suggest and your own imagination to see what you can do. Giving a card is so much more special when you can say you made it yourself!

5

Be prepared

Here is a collection of things you will need to make the cards in this book. You can collect things gradually and store them in a large box.

Tips

* Always read the instructions completely through BEFORE you start.
* Clear plenty of space to work.
* Always try laying things out before you glue them down.
* Take time to think about your ideas. If you get stuck, flip through books or magazines for inspiration, or discuss your ideas with a friend.

Things to collect

A craft knife and cutting board—always ask an adult to help you when using a knife

Pencil sharpener

Eraser

Hole punch

Craft glue

T-square

Double-sided tape, masking tape, and sticky pads

Tracing paper

For cutting and pasting: a variety of tagboard and papers (different colors and thicknesses), foils (sticky-backed if possible), colored tissue paper, scraps of shiny or holographic wrapping paper, scraps of fabric with interesting textures.

Glitter glue

Glue stick

Wax crayons

Scissors

Felt-tip pens, ballpoint pens (see opposite)

Gel pens

Pencils

6

Other useful odds and ends:

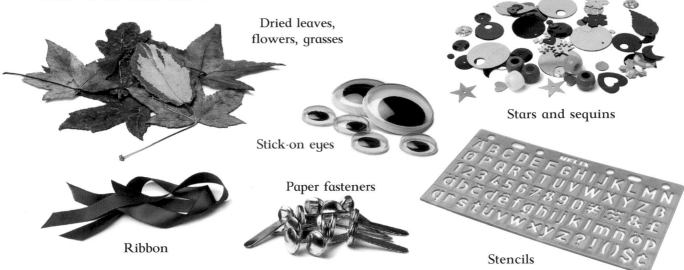

Dried leaves,
flowers, grasses

Stars and sequins

Stick-on eyes

Paper fasteners

Ribbon

Stencils

Useful techniques and ideas

✱ To cut straight lines, use a lined cutting board, or tape some graph paper onto a board. Line your work up with the squares on the board and use a T-square or ruler to mark or cut lines.

✱ Score the folds of each card by using an empty ballpoint pen case (remove the ink tube and nib). Run the pen down the side of a ruler to keep the line straight. Then fold the card and press down.

You don't have to be an expert at drawing to make these cards! Instead you can:
✱ Trace over pictures from books or magazines.
✱ Cut out pictures from magazines or wrapping paper.
✱ Draw stick figures.
✱ Draw simple patterns.

Here's MY card

Some people carry business cards as an easy way to pass on their business details to new contacts. In some parts of the world, people give cards with their personal details to their friends.

Look at this!

This design is very simple, but it isn't as easy to make as it looks.

dci
decorated cakes inc
Icing House
Butter Lane
Devon DV20 7ML

Telephone: 019-275-02840

✱ What do you notice first when you look at the card?

✱ How else could you use a second color?

Design and select

Design a personal card for yourself. Think carefully about how much information you will include. Sketch some simple pictures of yourself. Look at letters and numbers in old magazines and cut some out.

Challenge
What other image could you use on your card?

Make

1 Use masking tape to secure a sheet of tracing paper over some graph paper. With a pencil and ruler, mark the size of your card on the tracing paper. Make it no bigger than 3.5 inches (9 cm) long and 2 inches (5 cm) high.

3.5 in

2 in

2 Use the graph lines to draw a border, if you are using one. Cut out the picture you drew earlier and select letters and numbers from the ones you cut out. Place your picture and the words and numbers under the tracing paper; spell out your name and any other information you want on your card.

0033 377 7667

A few points to think about

- Try to leave plenty of space between the card edge, or border, and your picture or lettering.
- Make sure the letters are evenly spaced
- Make sure the lettering is not too close to the drawing.

3 Experiment with the picture and words until you are happy with your layout. Then, go over the design in pen on the tracing paper. Don't draw the very edge of the card; just mark where the corners are. Once the ink is dry, you can erase the pencil lines and admire your design.

Challenge
How else could you put lettering on your card?

4 Ask for permission to use a photocopier to make eight copies of your design. Carefully cut out your cards, using the corner marks as a guide, and attach them to a stronger piece of tagboard. Now, cut out your finished cards. Your friends will be impressed!

Challenge
Can you think of a way to use a second color on your card?

9

Nature card

You don't have to draw at all to make an impressive card. Instead, use natural things like leaves and grasses, but take time to get your design just right.

Design and select

Collect a selection of leaves and grasses. Place them on plain tagboard first to figure out how you will arrange them. Then, select the paper you will use. We've chosen handmade paper with rough edges to match the natural theme, and then mounted it onto stronger tagboard.

Make

1 Prepare your materials. We used dried grasses and leaves. To press them, put them between sheets of paper towel with a pile of heavy books on top. It takes a couple of weeks to dry the leaves.

Challenge
How else can you preserve leaves or flowers?

2 Cut out a rectangle of tagboard twice the size you want your card to be. Score down the middle using a ruler and an empty ballpoint pen.

3 Cut your handmade paper so that it fits over the front of the card, and glue it on.

4 Decide where the leaves will go and how you will attach them to the card. We cut small holes in the leaves and the front of the card. Then we loosely knotted the grasses, threaded them through the holes, and secured them with tape on the inside of the card.

Challenge
What could you use to make the leaves shiny?

Fold and fold again!

You can make a card really stand out by simply folding it in three. Use it for a party invitation; you can even make a detachable reply slip!

Design and select

Design a card that folds into three sections. Use a simple shape to create an effective pop-out image. Think about how you will use color, and sketch out some ideas.

Make

1 Divide a long piece of tagboard into four sections by drawing three lines from top to bottom. Make sure the sections are all the same size. Draw your design so it crosses the first line you have drawn.

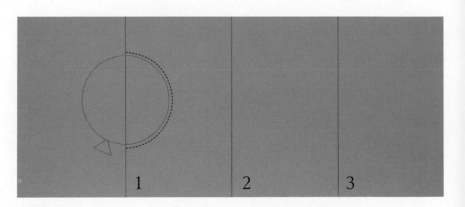

2 Score all the way down the middle line (2) using an empty ballpoint pen. Now score down the first line (1) above and below your design, but not through it. Then, ask for help to cut carefully around the right-hand side of your shape, as shown (left).

3 Next, decorate your picture. We cut a circle and a small triangle out of holographic foil to make the balloon shape, and glued them on.

4 Fold the card down the first and middle lines and try your pop-up. Mark the third line to show that it is detachable and to make your reply slip. We used a gold pen to draw a dotted line.

Challenge
We used the fourth section to make a reply slip. How else could you use this section of your card?

5 Write your message on the card— perhaps use a stencil for the important words. To avoid mistakes, it's a good idea to stencil onto some white tagboard first, then cut out the words and glue them onto the invitation.

6 If you decide to mark lines to write inside the invitation, be careful to draw them lightly in pencil first so you can erase them if you make a mistake. Finally, try out the full effect!

Cuddly cloth card

A fabric card always looks special. Here's how people make them in Bolivia, South America.

Look at this!

Bolivia is famous for its colorful textiles. This card was handmade using a frame to create the shape of a dove on the fabric.

✳ How do the colors chosen help the image to stand out?

Design and select

Make a card using soft fabric and a shaped frame. First, choose your fabric. Try out a few sketches and choose your shape. Simple is best! We've made a card for a new baby.

Make

1 Cut a rectangle of tagboard the size you want your card to be. Draw your shape onto the card, leaving about an inch (2.5 cm) between the drawing and the card's edge.

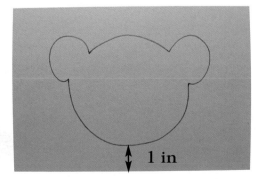

1 in

2 With an adult's help, use scissors to cut your shape out of the card, then discard the middle. Next, use a gold pen to draw around your shape to outline it.

14

3 Cut a rectangular piece of fabric larger than the shape and just smaller than your card. Put a thin layer of glue on the card and press it gently onto the fabric.

4 Now add facial features to the bear. Use different-colored material to make the nose and ears and secure them using a thin layer of glue. Add some plastic eyes above the nose.

Challenge
How could you adapt this card so it is padded?

5 Attach the frame to a folded piece of tagboard so that it can stand up. Cut out a piece of tagboard that, when folded in half, is a little larger than your fabric frame. Attach the fabric and frame to the card using double-sided tape. Using a gold pen, draw a thin border around the card to finish it off.

Challenge
Use this technique to make a colorful Hanukkah card.

Photo frame card

Do your parents send photos of you to your relatives? Why not turn them into greeting cards?

Design and select

Design a photo card to send to a relative; include a short message on the front. Look at some photographs of yourself; which one will work best as a card? How will you add your message?

Make

1 Put tracing paper over the photograph and lightly mark the area you are going to use. Figure out how big your frame needs to be and mark the corners of your photograph, as shown above. We also added a speech bubble shape.

Challenge
Make a funny card by experimenting with the words and photo. Can you make it on a computer?

2 Cut a piece of tagboard for the frame. It needs to be three times the size of the outside of your frame. Fold the tagboard into three equal parts.

16

3 Turn your tracing paper over and use masking tape to hold it in position on the middle section of the card. Draw over your tracing to copy the frame, bubble shape, and corners of the photograph onto the card. Make sure you get it the right way around. Remove the tracing paper.

4 Ask for help to cut around the frame and speech bubble using a craft knife, then push out the middle. Line up your photo with the picture corner markers and tape it in position. Seal the bottom and middle sections together with double-sided tape. Fold over the last section so that the card stands up.

5 Write your message on a separate piece of paper shaped like a speech bubble. Cut it out and glue it down. Draw a border around the photo using a gold pen. Write an additional message inside your card. Now your card is ready to send!

Challenge
How else could you decorate the frame?

17

A message with a bounce!

It's fun to send cards that move. We've used a simple technique to make this witch bounce up and down on her broomstick!

Design and select

Design a card with a part that bounces! Sketch out your idea and decide which part will move up and down. How will you make the bouncing mechanism? We made a Halloween card with a bouncing witch. Select your materials—we used tagboard for the witch and sequins for decoration.

Make

1 Trace the witch from your drawing onto a piece of dark tagboard. Cut out the main shape of your witch. Using different-colored tagboard, cut out separate pieces for the features, including the broomstick. Carefully glue them onto your witch.

2 Select tagboard for the background. Cut out a large piece of the tagboard, making sure the witch fits over the top.

Challenge
Can you give a shape to the background, too?

3 Next, take a piece of strong plastic (we used part of a thin plastic file used to hold paper) and cut it into a short strip. Bend the strip in half and press it down so that the two parts stay slightly open.

Challenge
The folded plastic makes the witch bounce. Can you think of another way to do this?

4 Using sticky pads, connect one side of the plastic strip to the witch and the other side to the tagboard.

5 Decorate the background of your card with cut-out shapes such as stars and moons. We used sequins for the stars and cardboard for the moon.

Challenge
Use this technique to make a "get well" card.

Pop-up card

A pop-up card makes your pictures come to life: simple designs work best.

Design and select

Design a pop-up card for a special occasion. Draw a picture of your idea. How will you add color to your picture? We made a card for someone who is moving to a new house.

Look at this!

You'll be surprised where you can find ideas! This children's book has a pop-up picture on every page.

✳ **How do you think the mechanism works?**

Make

1 Determine the size of your card and cut two pieces of flexible tagboard exactly the same size. Score a line down the middle of both cards using an empty ballpoint pen (see page 7). Put one piece aside.

2 With an adult's help, carefully cut two horizontal slits across the fold of the card using a craft knife. Make sure the slits are the same length and same distance from the edge of the card.

3 Score two lines down the card from either end of the slits to make a rectangle shape in the middle. Fold the card in half, pushing the rectangle inside the card.

4 Measure the card and draw your picture to fit it. Cut out the picture. Add any background details on the card, then glue your picture to the pop-up rectangle.

5 Attach the second piece of tagboard that you set aside earlier to the back of your pop-up to finish it off. Now you can add your message!

Challenge
Design a peephole through the front of the card that gives a hint of what's inside.

Good luck in your new home

Easy batik

Sometimes you need to make lots of identical cards, such as Christmas cards, party invitations, or thank-you cards. Here's a quick and easy way of doing it.

Look at this!

Look at this Indian Christmas card, which uses a technique called batik. Batik is made by painting wax pictures on fabric. When the fabric is dyed, the waxed parts don't absorb the color.

✳ How do you think the wax is applied?

Season's Greetings

Design and select

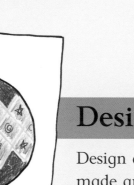

Design a simple-shaped card (we've made an ornament you can hang on a Christmas tree) and choose some colored tagboard. Sketch out a pattern to decorate your card. To create a batik effect, we've used wax crayons and thinned paint.

Make

1 Cut the main shape out of tagboard and use a hole punch to make a hole in the top so it will hang. Use your first shape as a template so you can cut out as many cards as you need.

2 Take a couple of sheets of good-quality paper. We chose white writing paper. Select a variety of wax crayons and try them out on the paper. Try different colors and shapes to make patterns.

22

3 Use paint that has been thinned with water and lightly cover the patterns with it—really experiment. Then, when you are satisfied with the effect, paint a whole sheet.

Challenge
How could you adapt this technique to make a picture card instead?

4 Cut interesting shapes from the patterned paper and glue them to your cut-out cards. We added a few dabs from a glitter pen to make the ornament sparkle.

5 Thread some gold ribbon through the hole in the card. Write a greeting on the other side. Now your friends can hang it on their tree!

Challenge
How would you make envelopes to fit these cards?

Spinning card

You can make a card with a moving picture using a rotating disk inside the card. We've created a flickering diya lamp to send at Diwali, the Indian festival of lights.

Design and select

Make a card with a moving picture. Sketch out your design and choose your materials. We used black tagboard, shiny tagboard, tissue paper, and a gold pen. Use a paper fastener to make the disk spin.

Look at this!

Candles are used for all sorts of celebrations, from religious festivals to birthdays.

✳ How can you make a card that flickers like a candle?

✳ Apart from Diwali cards, what other cards could you make featuring candles?

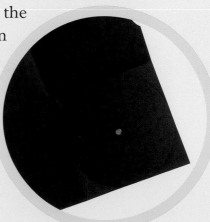

Make

1 Cut out a large piece of tagboard about one foot (30 cm) square. Using an empty ballpoint pen (see page 7), score lines down the tagboard to divide it into quarters, and then fold it up. Cut a small semi-circle out of the front edge.

2 To make the spinning disk, cut out a circle of thicker tagboard that is slightly smaller than your folded card. Ask for help to make a hole in the center of the spinner. Unfold the card and make another hole in the center of the bottom right section. Push a paper fastener through the hole in the spinner and the hole in the card and fasten in place.

24

3 With the card unfolded, figure out where your flame will go on the front and cut out a flame shape. Ask for help to do this.

4 To create the flame effect, cut out circles in shiny gold and red tagboard and glue them onto the spinner.

5 Cut out shapes to make the diya (the pot that holds a Diwali light). We cut the shapes from tissue paper and stuck them on with glue. Decorate the card with the gold pen. Now spin the card to make the flame flicker!

Challenge
How could you adapt this technique to make different pictures appear on the card?

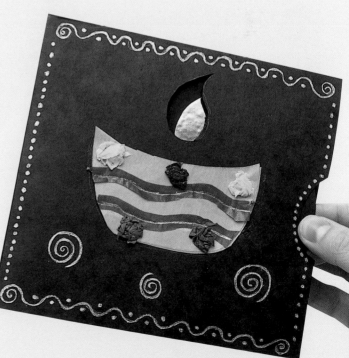

A card that grows

It's always nice to give flowers.
Here are some that actually grow!

Design and select

Make a collage card with flowers that really grow!
Cut out shapes and pictures that you like from old
magazines and newspapers, and arrange them in a
"patchwork" picture. Think about where you will
position your flowers and pots.

Make

1 Cut out a rectangle
of colored tagboard
and glue on the
background details. We
used different shades of
red to make bricks and a
window cut from a
magazine. Next, glue your
flower pots onto your
window sill.

Challenge
What else could you use
to make the collage?

2   Ask an adult to help you make a small slit at the top of each flower pot with a craft knife. Cut out T-shaped strips to attach the flowers onto.

3   Slot the strips of tagboard through the slits. Experiment with the position of the flowers on the front of the card. Do you want all of the flowers to grow to the same height?

Challenge
Could you make the flower grow tall enough to write your message on the stem?

Challenge
What else could you put on your card that grows?

4   Stick the flower heads onto the strips of tagboard and cut the strips to fit, leaving tabs at the top to pull the flowers up. Mount your design onto a large sheet of folded tagboard. Now you have a growing flower card!

A kissing card

People have been sending Valentine's cards for hundreds of years! This one has a special sliding mechanism. Pull the tab to make the couple kiss!

Design and select

Design a Valentine's card with a sliding mechanism. Think carefully about the materials you will need and sketch out a few ideas. We've used different colors and thicknesses of tagboard.

Make

1 You will need to cut out one piece of tagboard for the background of your picture, and a larger piece to make the folding part of the card. Decide what your background will be. We used a red heart on black tagboard.

2 Use a long piece of tagboard to make the sliding mechanism. Fold the tagboard in half lengthwise, draw an L-shape, cut it out, and glue the two sides together.

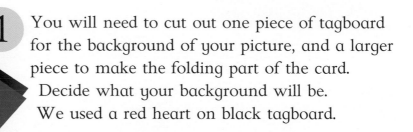

3 Draw, color, and cut out your two faces. Glue the boy onto the background card. Place the girl's face in position, but don't glue it down.

4 Cut a slit for the sliding mechanism in the background picture. To figure out the length of the slit (C), you need to measure the width of the tab (A) and add this to the distance between the lips (B). Remove the left face before cutting your slit with a craft knife. Ask an adult to help with this.

5 Place the long section of your L-shape behind the background and push the short part up through the slit. Glue a strip of tagboard along the bottom of the mechanism to hold it in place.

Challenge
How else could you make sure the mechanism is held in place?

6 On the front of the card, glue the girl's face onto the short part of the L-shape. Pull the tab to make sure the faces meet but don't overlap. Use double-sided tape to attach the background to the main folding card; make sure you don't stick the tab down as well. Now you can add your decorations.

Challenge
Can you reverse the slide effect to make an Easter card with an egg that hatches?

Glossary

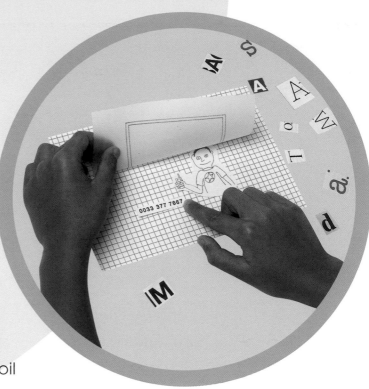

adapt
make suitable for your purpose

collage
picture made by putting together scraps of paper and other things

detach
to remove something that was attached to something else

diya
clay lamps containing a candle or oil used in Diwali, the Hindu festival of lights

e-card
an electronic card that can be sent in an e-mail

feature
detail; an important part of something

Hanukkah
a Jewish festival held in December

holographic
something that appears to be three-dimensional

inspiration
something that gives you ideas

layout
the arrangement or design of something

mount
to put a picture onto a piece of colored paper, or into an album

stencil
a piece of tagboard with pieces cut out of it; it is used to make a picture or design

textiles
different types of cloth, such as wool, nylon, or denim

Further information

You might find these Web sites helpful for finding ideas, techniques, and materials:

www.emotionscards.com/ museum/museum.html
A virtual museum of historical greeting cards. Looking at some ingenious cards from the past can give you ideas for the present.

www.thegardener.btinternet.co.uk/ preserving.html
Includes a number of ways you can preserve flowers and leaves— ask an adult to help you!

www.webindia123.com/craft/ paint/batik/batik.html
Information about how Indian batik is made, and a few samples.

http://cgee.hamline.edu/see/ goldsworthy/see_an_andy.html
Visit this artist's Web site to find more ideas for using natural materials.

www.crayola.com
Visit this site for craft ideas, to view new craft materials and find out where to buy them, and to create your own e-cards.

www.pbskids.org/zoom/ activities/do
Activities section includes some fun projects on greeting cards.

www.wipapercouncil.org
A Wisconsin paper site. Learn about paper and make your own recycled paper to use as stationery, drawing paper, or greeting cards, using materials from around the house.

www.elmers.com/index.asp
This site contains materials, ideas, and projects for different types of crafts.

Every effort has been made by the publishers to ensure that these Web sites are suitable for children and contain no inappropriate or offensive material. However, because of the nature of the Internet, it is impossible to guarantee that the contents of these sites will not be altered. We strongly advise that Internet access is supervised by a responsible adult.

Index

First published in 2005 by
Franklin Watts, 96 Leonard Street
London EC2A 4XD

Franklin Watts Australia
45-51 Huntley Street, Alexandria, NSW 2015

This edition published under license from Franklin Watts. All rights reserved.

Copyright © 2005 Franklin Watts

Editor: Rachel Tonkin; **Art Director**: Jonathan Hair;
Design: Matthew Lilly and Anna-Marie D'Cruz; **Photography**: Steve Shott
Picture credits: Mary Evans PL/Alamy: 4tr. Popperfoto/Alamy: 5t. V & A Images/Alamy: 4bl.
With thanks to Patricia Greathead for the loan of the cards on pages 5, 14, and 22.

Published in the United States by Smart Apple Media
2140 Howard Drive West, North Mankato, Minnesota 56003

U.S. publication copyright © 2007 Smart Apple Media
International copyright reserved in all countries. No part of this book may
be reproduced in any form without written permission from the publisher.
Printed in the United States of America

Library of Congress Cataloging-in-Publication Data

Greathead, Helen.
Cards / by Helen Greathead.
p. cm. — (Design and make)
Includes index.
ISBN-13 : 978-1-58340-955-8
1. Greeting cards—Juvenile literature. I. Title.
II. Design and make (North Mankato, Minn.)

TT872.G72 2006
745.594'1—dc22   2005051616

2 4 6 8 9 7 5 3 1